MW01227749

Adventures of the Miracle Man

God's overcoming love is captured in the pages of this journey that Jesus walked through with Bill. Chronicled by his beloved wife, Barb, the nightly exploits will let you see how personal and fun the Lord really is and how much HE cares about everything that concerns our lives. Bill's love and concern for his dear wife was always included in his "talks with God." Christ truly was the unbreakable strand in the center of their marriage which kept them rejoicing and praising Him in the midst of hospitals and pain. A must read for anyone who calls "their hospital" home away from home.

—Debra A. Holland, Director of Ministries,
The King's High Way

"It is God to whom and with whom we travel, and while HE is the end of our journey, HE is also at every stopping place."
—Elisabeth Elliot

We all have times in our lives when we're in need of a miracle…
times when we wait for God to do what only He can do. In
our times of waiting, our faith can be bolstered by hearing the
testimonies of others' miracles. From one of the most difficult
times in her life, Barb Hollace shares of the miracles she and
her husband, Bill, experienced to encourage you as you wait for
your miracle.

—Dr. Michelle Bengtson, www.DrMichelleB.com
Board certified clinical neuropsychologist,
Author of the multi-award-winning *Hope Prevails: Insights
from a Doctor's Personal Journey Through Depression,* and
Breaking Anxiety's Grip: How to Reclaim the Peace God Promises

Adventures of the Miracle Man will engage and encourage you.
Get ready to be empowered that no matter what adventure you
may be on, "God is still in control of what seems to be out-
of-control to our human eyes." Let these words echo in your
mind, "Don't give up! Bill got up every day, faced the enemy,
and determined he would win with God's help. You can do the
same!"

This book is amazing and miraculous!

—Sheri Powell, Christian author, speaker, counselor,
Founder and President of Pausing With God Ministries, Inc.
(PausingWithGod.com)

Whether walking on the hot sand of the desert or fighting spiritual battles in his dreams, Mr. Bill learned the lessons that those who are privy to the hard places yield, "Bad is good if you trust in God."

It is only a true insider that can espouse the nuances of God's economy – Mr. Bill's dreams and visions assure us he was one. Thank you, Mr. Bill. Thank you, Barb. Because of the faithfulness to your callings, many will know God in new and exciting ways.

—Dawn E. Stephenson, Founder and Director,
Kairos Coaching and Consulting

Once again, Barbara, has hit the mark in leading the reader closer to God through her personal and transparent journey during Bill's final walk with his Creator. The insights shared instruct the reader in drawing closer to God. I found the book illuminating of the darkness and faith building as well.

—Keitha Story-Stephenson PhD, SkyBlue Family Ministries,
BlueSky Wellness Center, Paradise, Texas

ADVENTURES OF THE MIRACLE MAN

Other Books about Bill's Journey

Yes, God! Volume 1

Daily Devotionals

Our Walk of Faith: The Journey to Bill's Healing

God's Grace on the Winding Road: The Journey to Bill's Healing

Miracle Man Trilogy

#1 Musings of the Miracle Man: Words of Wisdom Words of Hope

#2 Adventures of the Miracle Man: Dreams, Visions & Miracles

#3 Lessons of the Miracle Man: (Coming Fall 2021)

Adventures

of the Miracle Man
Dreams, Visions & Miracles

Barbara Hollace

Published by
Hollace House Publishing
Spokane Valley, Washington

Adventures of the Miracle Man: Dreams, Visions & Miracles
Copyright 2021 Barbara J. Hollace

For more information or to contact the author:
Email: barbara@barbarahollace.com
Website: www.barbarahollace.com

THE HOLY BIBLE, NEW INTERNATIONAL VERSION®, NIV® Copyright © 1973, 1978, 1984, 2011 by Biblica, Inc.® Used by permission. All rights reserved worldwide. The Living Bible copyright © 1971 by Tyndale House Foundation. Used by permission of Tyndale House Publishers Inc., Carol Stream, Illinois 60188. All rights reserved. The Living Bible, TLB, and the The Living Bible logo are registered trademarks of Tyndale House Publishers; [*Scripture quotations are*]from the Revised Standard Version of the Bible, copyright © 1946, 1952, and 1971 the Division of Christian Education of the National Council of the Churches of Christ in the United States of America. Used by permission. All rights reserved.

Book cover design: Christine Dupre, www.vidagraphicdesign.com
Book design: Russ Davis, Gray Dog Press, www.graydogpress.com
Book editing: Barbara Hollace, www.barbarahollace.com
Photography credit (Barb): Megan Kennedy, Rogue Heart Media
Photography credit (Bill): Jordan Caskey JC Media LLC

ISBN: 978-1-7345159-7-8

Printed in the United States of America

Dedication

To those walking out
their own "life adventure"
~you are never alone.
God Himself will come down
and walk with you.

"In the last days," God said,
"I will pour out my Holy Spirit upon all mankind,
and your sons and daughters shall prophesy,
and your young men shall see visions,
and your old men dream dreams."
~ Acts 2:17 (TLB)

Foreword

God came down to earth to meet an ordinary man on this extraordinary journey. Bill's journey was not defined by his illness or medical conditions but rather by the grace and mercy of God.

Bill commented that on this "adventure", God gave him a whole new perspective. He wasn't the only one who was touched by God on this journey. As their pastors and friends, we, as well as our congregation, were given an opportunity to stretch our faith and prayer life.

The tenacity of Barb's faith was exhibited as she fought for Bill's life by reaching out to God as well as recruiting a "small" army of believers to stand guard and pray, pray, pray!

Each day "we" received an update and a point of attack in prayer against whatever was attacking Bill at that moment in time. We saw miracle after miracle as the days went by with each situation conquered through the blood of Jesus.

Not only was Bill's physical healing journey an "awe and wonder" but the spiritual transformation that took place gave testimony to the goodness of God. God was no longer distant, the "man upstairs", Bill now knew Him more intimately as His Savior, Redeemer, and Friend.

As you read about Bill's dreams in this book, all that walking in a variety of terrains, it's like God was raising Bill up spiritually and teaching him how to walk in the Spirit. By squeezing years of fellowship, walking with God, into a very short time, He was preparing Bill for his journey into another realm.

During this time, Barb was also being prepared for a new place in her life. God raised her up to a new level as an intercessor and also taught her how to "swim" – to stay afloat, without Bill, knowing that God would always be there for her.

Bill's love, care, and concern for his wife is a golden thread woven throughout their journey as well as Barb's presence at her husband's side offering hope, support, and trust in a God who loved them both. What a blessing to see how our love for each other can grow in the refining fire of adversity.

And as the final chapter of Bill's story came to a close, it is not Bill or Barb that stands out as the central figure, but it is God, our heavenly Father, who walked with Bill not only here on earth and in his dreams, but now walks with Bill in eternity.

To God be all the honor and glory,

Dave & Alice Darroch
Senior Pastors, Spokane Dream Center

Introduction

What is an Adventure?

The dictionary defines adventure as "an undertaking usually involving danger and unknown risks." Sometimes adventures are sought out by us, and other times, they land in our laps unexpectedly.

My husband, Bill, and I embarked on an adventure that began January 10, 2018, the moment the EMTs arrived at our home early that morning. It would begin an unexpected five and a half months in five hospitals in two states as Bill recovered from multiple health challenges. The truth is God had a plan for this adventure long before we had a clue.

A health adventure has many twists and turns, unexpected places, sheer cliffs seemingly without a guardrail, and even wild flowers that pop up here and there. The difference in having an adventure with God is that He is still in control of what seems to be out-of-control to our human eyes.

Bill and I were blessed on our journey to his healing when God opened the windows of heaven and allowed us to peek in. This book you hold in your hands, *Adventures of the Miracle*

Man documents some of Bill's dreams and visions, and yes, the miracles that came from God's hands and God's heart.

The nickname "Miracle Man" was given to Bill because of the many times that God miraculously intervened and saved Bill's life. Not just once, but many times. So to honor those miracles and give tribute to God who graciously touched our lives, I am writing the Miracle Man trilogy.

The first book in the series is *Musings of the Miracle Man: Words of Wisdom Words of Hope* that pairs Bill's words describing his journey with the Word of God and God's promises that never failed. This second book, *Adventures of the Miracle Man: Dreams, Visions & Miracles* describes Bill's encounters with God, Jesus, angels, and others during his sleep. The third book will be *Lessons of the Miracle Man* summarizing what Bill learned on this journey.

During an interview, Bill described his healing journey in this way, "With this adventure, that's what I keep calling it now, an adventure, gave me a whole different perspective, that's not a building [the hospital], that's people – they care, they care."

In November 2018, we were blessed when MultiCare Hospital chose to use Bill's story to roll out two new programs, the Pulse Heart Institute and Neuroscience Institute, since Bill had both heart and neurological issues after the brain bleed. Bill was such a trooper to submit to a couple of hours of filming to create a three-minute video showcasing our story. (Tragedy & Triumph, Jordan Caskey, https://www.youtube.com/watch?v=PT-uw0LPdmQ)

Before God took Bill home to heaven in April 2020, on several occasions, He "strongly encouraged" us to share our story for His glory. As an author and book editor, it is such a blessing to share Bill's story with you all.

This book is not a book about dream interpretation or a theological study, but rather our humble offering to God as we share the "word of our testimony" through Bill's dreams and visions as I wrote them down right after each heavenly encounter.

My prayer is that you will be encouraged and that this book will turn your eyes toward heaven as you thank the Lord for being so good to us.

"Bless the Lord, O my soul, and all that is within me, bless His holy name." ~Psalm 103:1 (RSV)

Blessings,

Barbara Hollace

Contents

1.10.2018

The Day Our World Changed Forever...

Early on the morning of January 10, 2018, I woke up and discovered Bill struggling to catch his breath. His mottled skin verified that Bill was in trouble.

Calling 911 to get help along with crying out to God to save Bill's life and restore his breath was my two-prong attack against the enemy that we faced.

The diagnosis was pneumonia and Bill's heart was in afib [atrial fibrillation]. That night while in ICU, Bill had a heart attack. Three days later, he came down with Influenza A, and the next morning had a brain bleed that necessitated transfer by the LifeFlight crew to another hospital for brain surgery to remove the pool of blood.

It is miraculous that Bill survived those first five days. This would only be the beginning of our journey. Fifty days in ICU followed as multiple other things went wrong. The fight for his life continued even while he was sedated and the doctors held out little hope for his recovery.

I believed in the impossible. I believed in God. God can do mighty miracles – saving my husband's life was not too hard for God.

Recruiting prayer warriors from around the world to pray for Bill, they asked others to pray as well. My daily posts of our journey on Facebook and the impact of Bill's healing miracles continued to spread.

Many times, it seemed like the end of the road, but God would say, "No. It's not time. Bill's mission on earth isn't completed yet."

Our journey expanded across the state line into Idaho, where Bill was weaned off the ventilator and had his trach tube removed. After hitting a couple of more snags in two more hospitals, Bill finally came home on June 26, 2018.

His path to recovery continued through lots of hard work and wonderful people to help him on the journey. The most important message is this: Don't give up! Bill got up every day, faced the enemy, and determined he would win with God's help. You can do the same!

Dreams, Visions & Miracles

2018

You are the God of miracles and wonders!
You still demonstrate your awesome power.
~ Psalm 77:14 (TLB)

Bill's First Vision: January 2018

Early in Bill's journey, he was at a crossroads between life and death. We were not able to pinpoint the exact date this happened, but we know it was after his transfer to the second hospital.

Bill had a vision that is important to his story. What follows is Bill's best recollection about what happened.

[The narrative that follows is from conversations I had with Bill and pieced this vision together.]

I was in a dark place, a place between life and death. I was in a lot of pain. I struggled between wanting to die and wanting to live. There were moments when I just wanted God to end the pain but I didn't want to give Barbara up. I wasn't going to lose her.

Then I saw an open grave in front of me. As I looked down upon it, I knew it was my grave lying wide open. I was ready to go. Suddenly God was next to me and we began our conversation.

"Is Barbara going to be okay? Is there insurance so she will be okay financially? I won't go unless she is going to be okay. The pain is so great. I just want to go."

As Bill was speaking and looking at the grave, God blocked his path. Gradually, the grave began to close.

"What are You doing? I could barely get in there before and for sure I can't get in there now."

God replied, "It's not your time yet. There is work to do, move forward."

Bill watched as the grave closed completely.

"I'm no saint, Lord."

"All is forgiven, all is forgiven," God replied.

With God's parting words, the vision of the grave disappeared. God brought Bill out of the darkness little by little so "none of my parts would get messed up."

The journey to Bill's healing continued. It's not where we start but how we finish that matters.

Bill was hospitalized in five hospitals in two states between January 10, 2018 and June 26, 2018. Our records of his dreams and visions resumed after he was at home recovering.

9.1.18

God: "What do you want out of all this?"

Bill: "I want it all back [his mind]."

(Periodically, Bill gets a flashback of people and places – but no substance. "Sometimes I'm in the dark," Bill said, "a place of limbo, not life, not death.")

Bill: "Whatever is going to happen to my body will be big. I'm going into Wednesday, open-minded about my visit with the neurologist."

* * *

Bill: "At church, I was above them looking down. Someone was with me, not like anything before." (Everywhere I went, Bill could see me. Before the service, I was moving throughout the sanctuary greeting people sometimes out of his "natural" sight.)

Bill: "God reminds me He is changing me. It's very weird. It doesn't bother me as much as it did a month to six weeks ago. I know somewhere in my mind this will pass."

* * *

Bill asked about walking.

Jesus: "It will happen sooner than you think."

Bill: "I don't realize I'm walking until it's over."

God has a plan – slow and steady is the pace.

Bill's math: 1+1=3 because God is in the middle of it.

9.2.18

(Last night's dream)

From 7:30 PM to 9:30 PM, Bill, God, and Jesus were talking and so Bill didn't get any sleep at all.

Bill asked if I was getting enough sleep.

God: "Yes, she is as healthy as an ox."

Bill and I talked yesterday afternoon and he unloaded about 3 GB of data and now his mind is looking to be filled.

* * *

During the night, Jesus and Bill walked across three countries in the Middle East. Jesus told Bill it was good exercise walking in the sand.

Jesus: "Start off on your right foot to protect the bad one."

[The left one was affected by the brain bleed.]

At the end of the dream, four to five hours later, Jesus took off and left Bill on the sand.

Bill: "How do I get out of here?"

Jesus: "Follow that star."

And Bill ended up by the water.

(Jesus has quite a sense of humor and His laugh is almost deafening, according to Bill.)

* * *

Jesus told Bill that Baby Joanna [who was born with a hole in her heart] would be okay. Jesus put His finger out like "zap" to touch her heart. He also said that Bill would be walking sooner than he expected.

"The mission is almost ready."

9.3.18

Jesus had Bill walking all night again – over hills and valleys, all kinds of terrain. For a while, Jesus walked with him and talked with him.

Bill: "Where is Barb?"

Jesus: "She's sleeping – one of us needs to get some sleep."

[Bill during his daily naptime gets a rest.]

Bill told me that something big is about to happen because why would Jesus spend three nights walking with Bill showing him the world, if something wasn't about to take place?

Bill said God wasn't trying to build a house but to build a wall around us, around me to protect me. He is building His world around me.

Bill: "As the wall is built higher, Jesus elevates you higher so you are always on top of the wall, always within sight."

(Bill's legs are getting stronger; they didn't even hurt this morning after walking with Jesus all night.)

Bill and Jesus walked through the Middle East and other continents, not the United States. There were scenarios to avoid in the United States.

> When you pass through the waters, I will be with you; and when you pass through the rivers, they will not sweep over you. When you walk through the fire, you will not be burned;the flames will not set you ablaze.
>
> ~ Isaiah 43:2 (NIV)

Lessons from Last Night

1. Think and Listen. Jesus keeps bringing me up higher on the wall; Bill doesn't know what I'm seeing on the other side. I have a pivotal role that Bill doesn't know yet. God slowed us down so we can catch up. Jesus is building a wall around Bill and me to keep everyone out.

2. Jesus is telling Bill how to build the wall. He keeps building me higher. I'm on top of the wall. For Bill's benefit, Jesus is going slower to accommodate his healing - brain and leg. Bill grows and then Jesus sends Bill seeking more. Bill asks questions and Jesus answers. Looking forward to the neurologist visit on Wednesday. (Bill wonders at some point if I will be the one awake walking with Jesus while Bill sleeps.)

We're growing closer every day and people can see it stretching Bill without overwhelming his brain. Bill questions why the delay but each delay releases more understanding and God's plans.

Appointment with Dr. Melendez [neurologist] blew Bill away.

Dr. Melendez: "If you're willing to put in the time, you should be able to retrieve what you've lost. Your pacemaker supercharges your body."

Bill said, "What I can do and not do is up to me. Pacer is not a liability but an asset."

It gave Bill a whole new perspective.

It's like the desert to the Egyptians. Jesus didn't have a jet, He walked. It was His world and that's where He felt comfortable explaining things.

Dr. Melendez: "If you're looking to put in the time, go do it."

Bill: "When I want to, I can do it."

This afternoon during Bill's nap, Jesus said, "Forget the sand, recoup, and get ready to go on an adventure. The sand is to strengthen your leg."

Bill saw his doctor as able to condemn or condone what had happened and also about the hope to come.

One step closer to God – Bill has a new burst of energy today. The adrenaline is pushing again.

(This was Bill's first visit with a neurologist after being discharged from the hospital in June 2018.)

* * *

Jesus was sitting on the bed, but not there for long.

Jesus: "Now you're ready!"

Bill: "No. I'm tired."

Jesus: "I can get you un-tired."

[Bill didn't respond to Jesus' comment.]

Jesus: "Now things will slow down. Every step from this point on will lead you to your final destination."

9.6.18

(Bill spent last night walking and talking with Jesus.)

Whatever's going to happen is going to happen quickly. The gates will open up for 10 days but Bill has known that for a week.

Bill: "I think it's more than people realize. It's coming with a bang. God's going to turn the world on its axis. Not going to ask but will wait until I hear more."

Jesus told Bill that everything is okay physically after yesterday's doctor's appointment [neurologist]. Whatever is coming, we are set up for it.

Bill: "God's given everybody ample notice, it's not all bad."

Bill and I are not going anywhere. God will protect us while all this is going on.

God: "Sit and be quiet."

God is prepping us for something long and drawn out.

* * *

The trip to the Middle East wasn't a major thing. The sand is constantly moving. What's here today is gone tomorrow. To feel the sand underneath you, you have to have feeling in your feet.

Bill didn't leave tracks in the sand when he was walking with Jesus. When Bill was walking with Jesus, he didn't have any feeling in his feet. After yesterday, Bill has feeling in his feet again!

(The brain bleed resulted in a loss of feeling in his feet, but God just reversed that. Hallelujah!)

* * *

Bill was in the United States last night as he walked around with Jesus, just not in the big cities. Jesus told Bill what could happen but God still gives us the right to choose.

* * *

The right side of Bill's eye is healed and has been for 48 hours. With each passing hour, it is getting stronger.

(For the first six weeks after Bill's brain bleed when he was in ICU, he was temporarily "blind." All Bill could see was gray shadows and then gradually the Lord started to heal him and bring back his eyesight. We have so much to be grateful for on this journey. Even Bill's peripheral vision was restored. Thank you, Lord.)

Bill: "Will it go away? I don't think so."

14

"I'm only along for the ride," Bill said.

His legs are pivoting from the knees – an improvement.

Jesus: "Make sure you bring Barbara with you."

Bill: "I don't have to be altogether but with what I have, I need to be able to move quickly."

Eyes and legs first. Then be able to scan [see] and move more quickly with the legs.

Will it expand? [The healing] – Probably.

Bill: "I don't have to question it, just accept it."

Jesus told Bill yesterday that things would start happening "rapid fire."

(All this started just since yesterday – the changes in eyesight, legs, and increased feeling in his feet.)

* * *

Bill: "Where do You want me to go?"

Jesus held His hand up.

Bill: "Where do You want Barbara to go?"

Jesus held His hand up.

Bill: "Where do You want us to go?"

Jesus pointed to the world.

Bill: "Will You lead us?"

Jesus: "Yes."

Bill: "Will we win?"

Jesus: "Always."

Bill said to me, "You have a name. Jesus called you by name, Barbara."

Bill: "What do You want us to do?"

Jesus: "Get your rest for your weekend. This too shall pass."

[Jesus only stayed for a little while.]

(I sent a note to our friend, Keitha, asking her if she'd seen Jesus when she had a vision of Jesus sitting on her bed. Keitha said "yes" and sent me a photo of Jesus, a very close image to how she had seen Him. I showed it to Bill this morning and Bill said "yes" that was how he had seen Jesus on Tuesday and Wednesday night.)

* * *

(Jesus also made an appearance today during naptime.)

Bill said that we have to be awful sure about what we're doing outside the apartment.

"Whatever is coming won't come like a tidal wave but like waves in the ocean. None of us will watch it as it comes because we are walking and the "wave" [what's coming] is building up behind us."

"It won't be bad but it will be earth-shattering to a small group of people. Most people won't pay any attention to it."

"When the die is cast, it will be too late."

Bill and I have protective wings [angel's wings?] around us – we are part of it but not part of it. We are to take care of us and not worry about anybody else.

Bill watches over me and we are not to worry about the neighbors. There will be a lot of turmoil going on.

Major changes will have been made during this period. Bill's job is to protect Barbara, who now has a name.

Bill: "The only outsider is you [Barb] and Jesus has brought you inside. Bad is good, if you trust in God. Bad is bad, if you don't trust in God."

"We have to get our house in order. Don't worry, just be you. You cover me and I'll cover you. Pick the people we are close to, not the people who do lip service. There will be some persons who will try and push their agenda. We have been well-groomed by the Lord to stand on the truth."

"It's not the worst of the worst yet."

"We need to take one step at a time. We are not in that much of a hurry."

"Be aware! It's not chaotic but we can handle it. I'm sure."

Jesus: "Bring Barbara in! You paid your dues."

Bill: "We both did."

All Satan's stuff was washed away by His [Jesus'] blood.

9.8.18

Bill said I was in his dreams from about 8:30 PM - 9 PM last night until he got up this morning about 5:30 AM.

Bill and Jesus and I were walking and talking [in Israel] and Bill said to Jesus, "Can You slow down so I can catch up?"

Jesus told Bill it was time for him to lie down and sleep.

Before Bill could ask where he was supposed to sleep, Jesus pointed, Bill looked around, and there was a carpet on the ground. Bill went over to lay down on it and fell asleep.

Jesus and I were walking with big strides and then we got on horses to ride off for a discussion.

Bill said to Jesus: "She doesn't know how to ride a horse."

Jesus: "How do you know that?"

Bill: "She told me."

Jesus: "Well, she's with Me."

[In other words, no problem.]

Bill: "She's going to have a sore butt tomorrow."

Jesus [looking back at Bill]: "Go to sleep."

Bill made a comment to Jesus about the nice Arabian horses that Jesus and I were riding.

Jesus: "They're the best in the world."

Bill: "Agreed."

Jesus: "I taught you well."

When Jesus and I returned, Bill asked what we talked about.

Jesus said it was His prerogative not to tell Bill that I would know when it was "time" which could be 48 hours – maybe longer. It would be God's timeframe.

9.14.18

God is downloading information into Bill like a computer while he sleeps at night. Bill said he could understand 500 words and 400 words were my name.

Early October 2018

Bill was in Scotland with Jesus and they were at the lake where the Loch Ness monster lives. Bill and the Loch Ness monster had interacted but the really amazing part was when Barb got on its back and we went diving under the water.

Bill to God: "But Barbara doesn't swim!"

God: "She does now!"

You will do the things you think you cannot do.

10.3.18

Bill had a nightmare about standing on the ledge of a rooftop and could feel the fan blowing on him. Bill knew he had to get away from the edge. It was like 30 to 40 stories high. I was behind Bill and told him to reach back his hand to me, to safety. It scared him.

It was like the enemy was trying to lure him out of bed to fall. But Bill knew it wasn't that far [to fall off the bed] but he could get bruised up. No weapon formed will prosper!

After that happened, Bill made a pit stop. I prayed for him and he lay down and went back to sleep. While Bill was sleeping, I asked my Facebook friends to pray because it was a spiritual attack.

At the end of the nightmare Bill heard a voice [God's voice?] saying, "It's time, time to move forward."

10.6.18

Last night Bill was out soaring in the spirit with God.

God: "Buckle up."

Bill: "Where's the plane?"

God: "I am the plane."

Bill and God went around the world several times – but they were going so fast it was difficult to see much. Bill said they seemed to stay away from the United States.

God said it was almost time for Bill to come out of his cocoon.

God: "You will still be a while longer with the O2 [supplemental oxygen]. You will have two more growth spurts, and then no one can keep up with you except Barbara."

Bill will continue to be the muscle – and no one will mess with Barb. Barb will be the diplomat. But when it's time for Bill to move into position since the diplomat mode didn't work – then she needs to get out of the way.

God also kept mentioning Bill's glasses will be the next thing to arrive and the new dentures won't be long after.

(Bill had told me a few weeks ago that after he got his glasses and dentures, he would feel like a new man. God knows the desires of our hearts. After all, He put them there. New glasses arrived November 2018 and new dentures were completed in January 2019.)

Bill and God interact differently – kidding around – "picking" on Bill. God said He speaks more reverently to Barbara.

(Bill used to tell people that if he "liked" you, he would "pick" on you. It meant teasing you, kidding around with you, like you do with a friend.)

The conversation continued between Bill and God.

God: "Barbara needs more sleep/rest." [Bill agreed.]

God: "Bill, the best thing for your fatigue is sleep. When you're tired, sleep."

They continued flying around the world.

God: "Don't trust the politicians – they can slow down My plan."

[Bill agreed about the politicians.]

* * *

God told Bill that in six weeks will be when it's time for Bill to speak but then also talked about Bill speaking next spring [Spring 2019]. It all depends on how things work out. God wouldn't share "insider information" with Bill.

(On November 21, 2018, the day before Thanksgiving, Bill and I filmed an interview with MultiCare Hospital about Bill's healing journey. Bill and I both talked about his time at Valley Hospital and Deaconess Hospital. They used Bill's story to kick off two new programs at MultiCare: the Pulse Heart Institute and Neuroscience Institute. There was a private showing at the Fox Theater in April 2019. (Just like God said.) And also in July 2019, Bill and I spoke at God's Golden Thread conference in Hayden, Idaho. We had no idea in October 2018 how prophetic this dream was when God said it was almost time for Bill to speak and start telling his story.)

* * *

God: "It's almost time for you and Barbara to move forward."

(God gave us a year to recuperate, a year of downtime, to enjoy each other and our time together.)

God: "Get Barbara to laugh more."

(Well, it was kind of a "serious" time. But as the Bible says, "A cheerful heart is good medicine." Proverbs 17:22 NIV)

God dropped Bill off and he landed back in bed.

God told Bill that He wasn't very good at flying this modern plane.

Quite an adventure!

> Trust in the Lord with all your heart and lean not on your own understanding; in all your ways submit to him, and he will make your paths straight.   ~ Proverbs 3:5-6 (NIV)

10.7.18

Bill met miracle baby Joanna Joy at church today. Tina [her mom] brought baby Joanna over to see Bill. He touched her on the wrist to feel and sense her heartbeat – God's life in her.

Bill said she will be okay. She has to go through some suffering first. Hearing is an issue for her. Bill said maybe hearing aids or it could be not a hearing issue at all but related to the medication she is taking for her heart.

When Bill touched her wrist, Joanna opened her eyes and looked directly at Bill. After Bill released her hand, she closed her eyes again.

(It was the reunion of two of God's miracle children. When God's healing hand touches you, your countenance changes, the glory of the Lord radiates out of you.)

10.9.18

There is a battle in Bill's mind and body, the enemy is trying to get him to give up but he won't – he can't.

(God has a plan and purpose for Bill's life and no weapon formed against him will prosper – none!)

Three-pronged attack

- First vision with open grave while in ICU at Deaconess Hospital. (January 2018) God: "No, I have plans for you."
- Bill dreamed something happened to me while I was in the office which is right next to our bedroom. He was trying to figure out how to get out of bed and come and get help for me. (Bill thought I'd had a stroke or heart attack because he couldn't hear me making any noise.) (Late September 2018)
- Bill was on the edge of a building. The devil was trying to get him to jump from 30 to 40 stories up. I was behind him and reached out and took his hand and got him to safety. (October 2018)

The devil is a liar. Declaring that Bill is healed and whole in Jesus' name. Hallelujah, amen!

10.13.18

God and Bill were walking in the Swiss Alps [snow], by the ocean, and then in the desert [sand]. Bill didn't have shoes on but he wasn't cold.

God is Bill's PT [physical therapist].

In the Swiss Alps, there was four to five inches of snow on the ground and Bill was using his cane walking slowly but surely.

God told Bill that he would walk with a cane for a while and then one day it would be gone!

(This is something I have believed all along. Thank you, Lord, for that promise and revelation.)

God: "The O2 [supplemental oxygen] assessment [at the V.A. hospital] next week will go well. You will need O2 for a little while longer. They won't completely cut you off right away."

God is in a good mood. He was laughing quite a bit.

God [enjoying watching us]: "You make a good team."

Bill: "You should know. You brought us together."

[The discussion continued.]

Bill asked God why that when Bill went through this illness and felt the pain in his body, why did I have to go through the hard times as well? Wasn't that double jeopardy?

God: "No. Bill, while you were sleeping, I was doing a work in Barb as well." [Yes, God was and still is.]

(As Bill said today 10/13/18, the people in the old neighborhood wouldn't recognize you, you are a new person).

God: "The Barbara from the past in your head isn't the person who she is today."

Bill: "That's for sure!"

10.14.18

(Bill's dream last night)

Bill, God, and I were at the ocean and we were running on the beach. I was running faster than Bill. I would run, and then let him catch up, and then run again.

Bill: "I didn't know you could run so fast!"

God was enjoying watching us – said we made a good team.

Bill was commenting to God about me running so fast and him not being able to catch up.

God: "When I tell her to run – she runs!"

It always protects, always trusts, always hopes, always perseveres... Love never fails. ...And now these three remain: faith, hope and love. But the greatest of these is love.

~1 Corinthians 13: 7,8,13 (NIV)

During the night, Bill said he heard me talking out loud while I was sleeping. He heard voices and realized it was me, but couldn't understand me.

Bill asked God: "Who is talking?"

God: "It's not you or Me, and Barbara's the only other one in the room."

Bill: "I can't understand her."

God: "I can. She's talking to Me."

Bill said that I was talking very fast in this foreign language. I stopped for a little bit and then started again.

Bill to God: "What's happening? Will it continue?"

God: "She's almost done. It will just be a few more minutes."

And it was. And I went to sleep and stopped talking.

Bill said it wasn't any language that he knew. Although he thought it might be ancient Hebrew.

(The anointing oil I put on both of us before bed was the Balm of Gilead anointing oil from Israel. God knows the way we take and how we communicate with Him in our prayer language, even in our sleep.)

Last night during the night when Bill woke up for a bathroom break, he said he was having a nightmare.

Bill said that I was driving a BIG semi-truck – that he had never seen a trailer so big! Bill was riding shotgun.

At first, Bill didn't want to go. He told God there were already two passengers, Barb and God. God said He would ride on the hood.

God: "Bill, you're riding shotgun."

So Bill got in and God was on the hood with the wind blowing in His face.

Bill said that I was driving really good – staying in between the lines.

Bill: "My little Barbara driving a semi-truck." It was hard to take in.

We were just getting going on our journey and there was another pit stop (for real) and Bill went back to sleep.

After Bill got up, the next morning, I recorded most of last night's story and then after I finished recording it I asked Bill for a description of the semi. He said it was the color blue like Mary wore [the mother of Jesus in a picture he had seen] and the white in her covering. The trailer was the same colors.

Bill wasn't sure what we were picking up – people? They couldn't have been alive because you couldn't hear any sounds coming from the trailer. God said we would get the interpretation in a few days or maybe a week. [I don't have a record of any interpretation if Bill received one.]

As I drove across the Atlantic Ocean, part of the truck was underwater [the wheels] but the top was above the water. God said He was bored and this was a joy ride.

Bill said that the DOT [Department of Transportation that regulates the trucking industry] would go crazy – driving a semi-that's over weight, an unlicensed CDL [Commercial Driver's License] driver, driving too many hours without a break. But we didn't burn any petrol – only God! At least there was no damage to the environment and I wasn't actually driving on the road but above it.

Bill said at one point God had me hit a button on the gear shift, and we went as fast as if we were flying! (A little like K.I.T.T. [a talking car] from the Knight Rider, television show in the 80s?)

* * *

When we were out for a drive today, we were sitting in the parking lot by Dairy Queen near Albertson's when a train went by. Bill said that the trailer attached to the semi I was driving last night was the length of 10 train cars – freight cars, but it didn't have the space between them, it was solid. Wow! That's really long!

(The significance to me about all this was that yesterday (Friday 10.19.18) when I got stuck at the train tracks at Trent and University, I was watching the train as it was slowing down and praying that it would make it through the intersection without stopping. I counted 10 freight cars before the last engine. God was preparing me for the mental picture Bill would provide. And then when the train did stop, it didn't clear the tracks far enough for the arm to lift. Another 10 feet would've done it. Three of us were stuck and not able to cross the tracks.

It was getting time for Bill's caregiver to leave so I called our former neighbor to go stay with Bill until I got home because it wasn't safe for Bill to be alone [too wobbly to move safely on his own]. The three of us who were stuck at the tracks, backed up, and got back onto Trent Avenue and I went home.)

Late October 2018

Bill to God: "Can I be President of the United States?"
God didn't answer him one way or the other.
Bill: "How about VP [Vice President]?"
God: "No."
Bill: "How about negotiator?"
God: "No."
Bill: "Barb would be good for that job."

God: "No. I have more important things for her to do. I'm not going to waste her talent on politicians."

God to Bill: "Why limit yourself to the United States?"

Bill said something to God about my wanting to work in the justice system in Washington DC but that didn't work out.

Bill: "You shot that down."

(Note: This had to be God – how else could Bill remember this? Most of his memory was lost after his brain bleed in January 2018. I would have originally shared this with Bill probably in late 1993 or early 1994 – 24 or 25 years previously. I attended Gonzaga Law School because of God's call on my life surrounding justice in the legal system.)

Again, the message is that our work for God will be worldwide – a recurring theme.

10.27.18

Early in the morning about 1:30 AM, Bill said something shifted – it was like his brain became fully functional – activated!

Spokane Dream Center [our church] was having all-night prayer on that Friday night, 10 PM to 5 AM.

During the day [following the all-night prayer session], Bill was fully engaged, bright-eyed with no additional oxygen needed while he was awake. Amazing and miraculous!

10.29.18

We worked on voting this afternoon and filled out our ballots – it was really hard for Bill. Bill said he had insider information from God. None of the people he saw on the ballot were in the dreams God showed him of the political situation. The only one who survived was Trump.

11.9.18

(We were notified that at the end of next week, Occupational Therapy will discharge Bill and Physical Therapy and Speech Therapy will give us a plan and materials to help us continue to get Bill stronger because our insurance time has expired. The physical therapist wants to come back in the spring [Spring 2019] and work with Bill walking outside.)

* * *

Physical therapy session: Bill walked backwards while using the four-wheeled walker.

Then by the sink, Bill walked forward and backward without holding onto the counter. Three sets, then a rest, and then two more sets.

It broke down the wall that Bill had mentally that he would always have to walk with a cane.

With God all things are possible!

11.10.18

Overnight Bill was dreaming that we were both running in the water. Bill was running after me and I would run ahead, and then stop. Then he would run toward me and sometimes fall, and then get up and not be hurt because he was in the water.

God was there for part of the time.

Bill: "But she can't swim."

God: "She can now. There are lots of things she can do now."

* * *

We were at the ocean. I was partially in the water but as we went to the shore, when I came out of the water, my bathing suit wasn't even wet.

I was challenging Bill to run on the sand.

Is this a preview of our time together doing physical therapy at home in the months ahead of us? Lord, You will direct our path.

> With man this is impossible, but with God all things are possible.   ~ Matthew 19:26

11.11.18

Last night, Bill was dreaming that he was running [chasing me on hardtop].

Bill said he didn't know I could run so fast.

In real-time, his legs were running in the bed. I noticed this when I got up at 5 AM.

11.17.18

Last night Bill was dreaming that the world was being destroyed all except for us.

God was leading us out of it.

God: "Don't look back. Just keep on going."

(This is a reminder of the story of the destruction of Sodom and Gomorrah in Genesis 19. Lot and his wife and family were told "not" to look back. Lot's wife looked back and turned into a pillar of salt ~Genesis 19:26.)

11.19.18 5:30 AM

Since about 2 AM, Bill and God were flying together. God was like a bird – no airplane.

God said to Bill, "Welcome back!"

2019

In peace I will lie down and sleep,
for you alone, Lord,
make me dwell in safety.
~Psalm 4:8 (NIV)

2019: Dream with Bill and Peter, Jesus' disciple who walked on water to Jesus.

Peter walked with Bill 10 to 12 times last night. He had a sword and handed it to Bill to carry.

[Peter was carrying three swords: left side, right side, and in the back.]

Peter: "Bill, don't let my sword hit the ground."

[Bill didn't believe that he was able to carry Peter's sword.]

Peter: "He [the devil] is a deceiver. He tries to scare you. The devil is not a pushover – look in his eyes and you can see it."

Peter talked to Bill about walking on the water.

Bill: "I'm too heavy to walk on the water."

Peter: "I'll be back again."

Peter to Bill: "Focus on the picture. Walk on the water." Peter spoke this as he walked down the hallway in our apartment.

[Bill describes Peter as having gray hair and a gray beard.]

Peter said, "I'm number one. Satan was number one but his ego got in the way. Now number two Peter is number one."

Bill: "You are more than my drill instructor."

Peter: "By the time I'm finished, you'll be up there with me. If I had my way, you'd have mastered this already. That's where our Lord is very patient."

Peter is not patient. Peter is God's go-getter.

God said to Peter, "Go grab Bill and bring him up here."

Peter: "You'll be on your way before you know it. How much time do you need to think? 22 minutes? Walking – it's really not that hard."

[Bill wasn't convinced that walking wasn't really that hard.]

Peter: "You haven't walked on your own for 15 months. Walking turns the corner. You just have to get stronger and closer to God."

(In our apartment after Bill came out of the hospital, he was doing physical therapy at home. One of the things the physical therapist was working on was having Bill focus on a point in the distance to help Bill stay "on track" and steady. I have a picture hanging on the wall at the end of the hallway of Peter coming to meet Jesus walking on the water. It was Bill's focal point. God is so good. Who better to teach you how to walk again than Peter who Jesus invited to step out of the boat and come to meet Him walking on the water? God was a vital member of Bill's rehab team.)

January 2019

Bill dreamed that I was driving some kind of semi-truck that was three times bigger than what he had seen in the previous dream where I was driving a semi with a trailer that was the length of 10 freight cars. The truck was as tall as our apartment building – two stories high.

Bill was with me. I could see this guy but Bill only saw a shadow.

Barb: "I'm going to run that guy over."

I went to climb up into this truck but I got winded [tired] just climbing up the stairs to the cab.

There was someone else on the ground besides this shadow – a buff guy that Bill said was an angel. When I first started up the truck, I couldn't shift the gears right. The angel climbed in on the driver's side and said, "I will do this for you."

Bill said that he knew that the "shadow" I saw was Satan and I was going to destroy him.

The truck ran him over and killed him. And when that happened, the angel said, "That bought God 72 hours."

1.5.19

(After Bill's nap this afternoon)

Bill said that I am the trigger – I will kick open the first door that will determine our path.

God: "Bill, back her play. There's nothing you can't do. Walk away from fear."

[Bill will back my play.]

Bill asked God: "Is she ready? Isn't she?"

God: "Once the gate is open, it's open. If the floodgates have opened, you have to hang on when the waters roll."

God to Bill: "You're in four different areas – you haven't moved six feet."

Bill to Barb: "Don't tell me you can't swim, you can! Figure out what you're going to do and not going to do. You don't have to jump on everything."

(God help me and give me wisdom.)

1.11.19

Bill woke up and all night was in snow – deep snow – trying to move it – he couldn't. Bill was surrounded by lots of people but couldn't find me.

1.12.19

Bill's dream from last night was that he was in the snow again but he looked to his left and I was waving at him, motioning him to follow me. I had cleared a path.

God had both hands raised and said, "Get it ready! Get it done!"

God called me, "Barbara Jean."

"It" was a publishing company. God has been sitting on lots of projects and was running out of room.

There was a lightning strike that barely missed Bill.

God told Bill that we are to go out for tea today to talk it over and then Bill needs to get out of the way so I can do my thing.

If I need help, there are lots of reinforcements that have been sitting around. When I start, it will flow very smoothly.

* * *

God: "On the political front, I hope the Democrats have a good sense of humor. My people are stupid talking about Congress. Trump has a place reserved for him in heaven."

God: "The world is walking in confusion." [They need what we have to offer. Set it up for us, not them.] (Follow God's instructions.)

1.13.19

On Saturday night, (1/12), Bill had a dream and there was a group of angels that were encouraging him to do more walking.

In the early part of the dream, we were on the beach by the ocean and I was running ahead of Bill and then I would let him catch up to me, and then run some more and laugh. Then I walked out on the water and he couldn't catch me.

The second part of the dream, the pack of angels headed up by the Archangel Michael said that they were tired of me [Barb] always winning and out running Bill. They had a plan to get him walking using both the regular walker and the Caddy [four-wheeled walker].

During the rest of the night, they had Bill walking all over the place. Bill was tired when he woke up but committed to doing more walking with a walker.

Bill said something about me not being able to swim. The Archangel Michael said, "She can swim now [and walk on the water]. If she can do that then you can walk!"

1.20.19

The bullet train from Japan is leaving the station and it has already run two cycles – it's about to pick up speed!

Last night God showed me the MultiCare Hospital video on one end and NIACH/RHN [North Idaho Advanced Care Hospital/ Rehabilitation Hospital of the Northwest] video on the other – just like the Alpha and the Omega, the Beginning and the End.

And God is calling us to fill in the section in the middle with writing and speaking.

The time is now.

Why are we waiting for a green light when God has already given us one?

> "God doesn't call the qualified, he qualifies the called." ~Mark Batterson *The Circle Maker: Praying Circles Around Your Biggest Dreams and Greatest Fears*

1.23.19

Bill had dreams about the MultiCare video [featuring Bill's story]. It was at church. Some guy Bill didn't know came up to him and said, "Thanks."

Bill had a puzzled look on his face.

The guy said, "It's the first time that I have seen the actual results of my prayers."

Then Katie and Julie came to Bill while the DVD was playing and held his hand while they watched it without saying anything.

They asked if he understood it.

Bill: "No, but they couldn't get started without me."

They said, "Oh, Bill!"

(After Bill's brain bleed and brain surgery and what followed including sedation and intubation, etc., Bill didn't remember the first few months. It bothered him at first when we talked about it but then God reminded Bill that he was asleep. And Bill finally had peace about it.)

1.27.19

We tried to play the DVD of Bill's interview today at church but there was trouble with the sound. The cable must be broken somewhere. Sounds like the enemy's tactics. The worship team leader's microphone wouldn't work at all either.

(Bill wanted to get up and walk out of his wheelchair this morning at church. He feels an urgency to get walking and will use the Caddy [four-wheeled walker] more this week.)

> "What do you want me to do for you?" Jesus asked.   ~Mark 10:51(TLB)

* * *

(Bill's dream last night)

Three times, God asked Bill, "Are you ready?"

Bill's response: "Ready for what?"

[Silence from God]

Bill finally said, "I can only walk a little."

God said, "That's minor."

God pointed out Bill had doubled his steps, just this week, during transfers.

Bill wants to know what he's getting ready for – to do what?

God: "Just trust Me."

2.2.19

Bill has had dreams three Friday nights in a row about destruction and God watching it happen and not stopping it.

Third week: Today, Bill destroyed a school and a church. The sunlight was finally coming through the darkness. Bill thinks this is where we will be and operate from this place.(The sunshine came out today when Bill and I went out, showing the manifestation in both the natural and supernatural.)

2.23.19

In the middle of the night, Bill had a dream that I won $67 million in the lottery with no taxes. I told Bill I didn't even buy a ticket. He rolled over and went back to sleep.

2.24.19

(Bill's dream last night)

It was a primitive environment and the people couldn't speak. They used hand signals. It seemed God's message was, see they can't even speak. They can move around but can't speak. "You can speak, Bill. Slow down and hold on. Hope is coming. Spring is coming."

Bill said he can also see things on the horizon coming – they seem to be speeding up. Bill can understand why Pastor Dave is concerned.

The worship team sang a song this morning about not being satisfied with the ordinary. We must give God our all.

2.26.19

God is angry but still merciful. Bill was in Germany in the concentration camps. God has him on a world tour teaching him strategies.

2.27.19

In Bill's dream, I was swimming in the ocean [the biggest swimming pool that God has].

Bill: "She can't swim."

God: "She doesn't know that she can."

God's message to Bill: "Sleep when you can because the time is coming when you will be very busy. The download starts tonight. The time for sympathy is over – it's time to sweat."

1. Belgian chocolates: [like the Hallmark movie: *Love, Romance and Chocolate*]

    They named a chocolate after me [Barb].

    Bill said, "She doesn't even like chocolate."

2. Africa: [Hallmark movie: *Love on Safari*] Bill was afraid that the animals would bite me.

God said, "Don't be afraid. Barb is okay. She will go anywhere that I tell her to go. She will go whenever I want her to go."

2.28.19

(Bill and God talking during the night)

Bill: "I am not defeated."

God: "Keep talking to Me."

God and Bill are just beginning a long journey together.

God: "Bill, drink more water."

(Bill has increased to two bottles a day – he still has a ways to go. But Bill is trying his best even though he doesn't really like drinking water. Bill was more of a "coffee" guy before all this started. He stopped coffee and cigarettes "cold turkey.")

3.2.19

The weather has been really cold like 5 degrees overnight with northeast winds making the wind chill -10 to -25 degrees.

* * *

God has been letting Bill sleep the last few nights.

God's message has been brief: "Sleep" and "Pray – I am with you."

3.9.19

Bill said that God let him sleep except they did have some conversations.

Bill: "Do we win?"

God: "I don't back losers. Yes, you win."

Bill asks God about walking – specifically walking with a cane.

God pointed out where Bill's cane was sitting in the corner and that it wouldn't be long before Bill would be using it. And that Bill would get his "strut" back.

Bill asked God about money.

God: "I'll take care of it."

Money will not be an issue, God will provide.

God said that Barb had two best-sellers written [I wish I knew which two they are].

3.17.19

God said He wouldn't be talking unless there was something to share. "It's under control, sleep, and then wake up."

4.5.19

During the night, Bill had a dream. I said that I was going out to take care of business and would be back in a while. I drew my sword when I left. I returned later having completed my mission – with no evidence of what happened on the outside.

[The sword refers to the "sword of the spirit" (Ephesians 6 – armor of God). At night I am using the Word of God to fight spiritual battles and win!]

4.6.19

In Bill's dream, God said, "Tell Barb to get all these books off My chest." There are more books coming and we need to get writing our own. Bill needs to tell me what he remembers – get started and do it.

4.8.19

Last night Bill dreamed that he was all over the place doing work for the Lord. God brought Bill to the outside of a pink house and asked if he remembered his military training.

God: "Destroy it."

Bill: "Is it one of Yours?"

God: "Yes. Don't look inside, just destroy it."

Bill destroyed the house using the weapons God provided.

Bill was tired when he woke up this morning.

(The air is thick with the spiritual warfare that surrounds our church's Easter drama production.)

4.19.19

Bill was dreaming of Jesus' crucifixion. Bill said that hasn't happened since his First Communion when he was seven years old, almost 70 years ago. It was so vivid, he was checking for nail holes in Jesus' hands.

[Message: That God has been near to Bill all this time. Bill said, "If it draws me nearer to God, it's worth it."]

2019: Sunday night

God called Bill's name. When God came close, God wrapped His arms around Bill and lay down and went to sleep next to us.

> In peace I will lie down and sleep, for you alone, LORD, make me dwell in safety. ~Psalm 4:8 (NIV)

8.1.19

Bill was dreaming last night and his mind was going all night. He was reviewing his life up to 120 years of age. At age 88, God said, "Slow down."

Bill asked God about me: "She's getting older."

God said, "She will be okay. You guys are a team."

8.4.19

The last four Saturday nights, Bill was riding a motorcycle in his sleep. Last night, Mémère [Bill's grandma; Mémère is French for grandma] made him drive it into the ocean.

Mémère said, "No more. Does Barbara know about this?"

Bill: "No."

Mémère: "Let's keep it that way."

10.15.19

God's word to Bill, "Listen!"

11.11.19

(Last night Bill and God had a talk – it's been a while.)

Bill: "Do I win?"

God: "Yes, you do."

God: "You are running thin on patience."

Bill: "Yes."

God: "I know – that's the way I made you. I am teaching you both patience."

God: "You will hear by the end of the week about the surgery."

Bill: "Will I be okay?"

God: "Yes, I have a surprise."

Bill: "What is it?"

God: "You know what the word "surprise" means, right? There may be some healing that's already done."

[Was it Bill's heart or hernia?]

God: "Rest."

Bill: "Is Barb sleeping?"

God: "Yes."

Bill: "She's getting more rest."

God: "Yes, I noticed. You've done a good job."

Bill: "I think she's at about 75%. Can you get her to 80% or 90%? That would be better."

God: "It's a work-in-progress. You win."

(God is completing what He started. Bill's heart stent surgery was scheduled for December 23, 2019.)

Turning Points

1. "Everybody thought I was going down but I heard you once and gave you two thumbs up." [Deaconess Hospital]
2. Bill walking with the walker.
   I said, "You can go further."
   Bill: "You were the first one I had to see."
   [NIACH – North Idaho Advanced Care Hospital, Post Falls, Idaho]
3. Barb staying at the hospital with Bill: "When I asked you [Barb], you stayed at the rehab hospital. If I rolled over at night, all I had to do was open my eyes and I could see you. And you were there. When I needed an ounce of courage, I could look and you were there."
   [Rehabilitation Hospital of the Northwest, Post Falls, Idaho]
4. Prayers with God:
   Bill: "God would listen and I knew that He was there."
   God: "Slow down, Bill. We'll take it one day at a time." [Three weeks ago]

5. Neurologist [Dr. Melendez] visit: "We did it! You [Barb] are part of the intricate system of my mind." Bill referring to Dr. Melendez's encouragement: "The sooner I get it done, the sooner I can walk with you."

> But this I call to mind, and therefore I have hope: The steadfast love of the LORD never ceases, his mercies never come to an end;they are new every morning; great is thy faithfulness.
> ~Lamentations 3:21-23 (RSV)

2020

Come to me, all you who are weary and burdened
and I will give you rest.
~ Matthew 11:28 (NIV)

1.15.20

Bill woke up and said he had been dreaming about shopping for "real clothes" for the last three hours in Boston and then New York City. Bill and I went by car and had a driver. Bill was buying three-piece suits and two-piece suits and good shoes – mostly tailor-made. Wow! [This shopping trip was about Bill, my turn would come later.] NOTE: In the dream, Bill was completely healed and whole – no brace, no limp, no need for oxygen, etc.

(Since January 2018 when Bill first went into the hospital, he had been wearing sweatpants and t-shirts or polo shirts. That was not Bill's usual attire. Bill was a "dapper" dresser. A suit, dress shirt, tie, and good shoes felt normal to him. Casual for Bill was rolling up the shirt sleeves on his dress shirt. What a blessing to have a "normal" moment even in his dream.)

1.23.20

Bill woke up about 3:15 AM to use the bathroom and told me that in his dream there were six people fighting the whole world. Bill and I were two of them.

We were both using our swords. It appeared I was more adept at it and deadly. With one swing, I was taking out half a block of people.

A beheading was involved using my left hand. [My left arm was sore this morning.]

Bill said maybe the other four were angels. We were winning although the odds were against us.

At one point in the dream, I was down and this guy thought I was dead. He walked past me, and I got up and took him out.

This is how we fight our battles with God's help and favor.

2.17.20

(Bill sharing with Barb during breakfast after a good night's sleep. He was at the Rehab Hospital recovering from his aortic valve replacement surgery.)

"I can see the top of the mountain. I haven't gotten over it yet but I can see it. I'm feeling the best I ever have. My systems seem to be lining up."

Bill was bright-eyed and ready to embrace the day.

"Live in fear or die happy." ~Mr. Bill

Bill continued to say, "I have been fighting fear. I need to have confidence in myself."

Have I not commanded you? Be strong and courageous. Do not be afraid; do not be discouraged, for the LORD your God will be with you wherever you go. ~Joshua 1:9 (NIV)

2.28.20

On the day before Mom's memorial service, Bill was taking his afternoon nap when God gave Bill a vision of Mom in heaven. Mom was walking around checking things out. God described her as the "new kid on the block." Mom replied that it was "a BIG block!"

Mom and Bill had a conversation that started with their familiar banter.

"Where's my donut?" Mom asked.

They both laughed.

[When we went to visit my parents, Bill would stop by the bakery on his morning walk to pick up a fresh maple bar for Mom. Mom loved maple bars!]

"And I don't want a maple bar."

[What? Mom not wanting a maple bar. That was strange.]

"What kind do you want?" Bill asked.

"I want one of those crème-filled ones," Mom replied.

[Bill must have had a puzzled look on his face.]

"Because here in heaven, I don't need to worry about my weight!"

And then she winked and laughed as only Mom could do.

Bill asked if Dad was going to be okay.

"Yes, Dad will survive," Mom reassured Bill. "And so will you."

[Bill wasn't expecting the comment about him.]

"Sleep!" Mom said to Bill.

"I am sleeping," Bill replied.

"No, you're not. You're listening to me. You need to tune people out – that's the secret. You're going to be fine."

[Sleeping has always been Bill's best healing strategy. It was easy to agree to those terms.]

"Take care of Barbara," Mom said.

"Barbara's taking care of me but that's going to change," Bill replied, confidently.

"Mom, is there anything I should know?"

"I'm in heaven!" she replied with a big smile.

[When Bill woke up from his nap, he shared this vision with me. Bill said Mom looked good, like she did before she got so sick.]

3.13.20

When Bill woke up this morning he said to me, "I didn't know you knew how to drive a train."

I replied, "I didn't know I could drive a train either."

Bill said that I was on the front of the train and had a lantern that I was waving back and forth and saying, "I need to shine the light so people can find their way."

Bill was on the train tracks running in front of the train. I was concerned that Bill was going to get run over by the fast-moving train.

Bill said that he would be fine.

The train was traveling on train tracks on flat land and there were train cars behind the engine that were filled with people.

3.14.20 (Second train dream)

Again, I was on the front of the train with God next to me. (Bill said all he could see was the light [glory of the Lord] and believed it was God. The train was much longer than last night. You couldn't see the end of the train because there were so many train cars filled with people. Bill wasn't sure about our destination.)

The train was moving very fast like a bullet train through the wind and the snow as we traveled over the mountains.

I kept telling people to get out of the way.

Bill was trying to out run the train. He was running ahead of the train on the tracks.

Bill said God was having some fun with him.

God said to Bill: "You're going to fall."

Bill said: "No, I'm not because You are here with me. When You are gone, it may be a different story."

After we came down off the mountain, where it was warm, the whole train disappeared.

Barb to Bill: "Hon, it's going to get better."

Bill: "When?"

Barb: "I can't tell you that but it will happen suddenly and take you by surprise."

(When Bill shared these two dreams with me, I thought it meant that with Spring 2020 coming quickly that God would finish Bill's healing and we would begin the ministry God had planned for us.)

4.19.20 The Last Chapter

God had a surprise for us. Any good mystery writer leaves you in suspense until the very last chapter. Well, God is the best author and creator that I know, and He had written a surprise ending to Bill's story.

Bill was recovering from his February heart surgery at home and regaining his strength. He often remarked about how strongly his "new" heart was beating with the new valve. "My heart wants to run but my body's not ready for that yet."

Daily, we saw improvement, better skin tone, and more light in his eyes. Bill was still contending with a rogue hernia that needed to be repaired once he recovered fully from the heart surgery.

And then God intervened in our story in a new way. Early the morning of Sunday, April 19, 2020, I woke up because Bill's breathing didn't sound right. Turning on the light, I discovered something was wrong and called 911.

The ambulance quickly took Bill to the hospital. As a friend drove me there, we prayed that I would be granted entry to be with him. During the 2020 COVID-19 pandemic, some hospitals were denying all guests.

However, the Lord opened the door for me to go in. The bottom line: Bill didn't have a heart attack or a stroke. In fact, they didn't know what was happening.

At 3:54 AM that morning, Bill's heart stopped beating for the last time on earth as he walked into heaven.

There was great rejoicing in heaven even as I was in shock, finding it difficult to grasp that Bill was gone.

There was no pain. There was no suffering in those final hours. The Lord was gracious because He loved Bill so much.

God had the final word. God Himself came to take His beloved Bill home. The nighttime visits were over. Now they would have time and eternity together.

From time to time, I hear Bill's laughter echoing down from heaven. His presence is always with me and God's hand of protection surrounds me.

Today, I give God all the honor and glory because He has done great things for us, He has done great things.

Favorite Scripture Verses

Have I not commanded you? Be strong and courageous. Do not be afraid; do not be discouraged, for the LORD your God will be with you wherever you go.   ~ Joshua 1:9

In peace I will lie down and sleep, for you alone, LORD, make me dwell in safety.   ~Psalm 4:8

You are the God of miracles and wonders! You still demonstrate your awesome power.   ~ Psalm 77:14

Bless the Lord, O my soul, and all that is within me, bless His holy name.   ~ Psalm 103:1

Trust in the LORD with all your heart and lean not on your own understanding; in all your ways submit to him, and he will make your paths straight.   ~ Proverbs 3:5-6

When you pass through the waters, I will be with you; and when you pass through the rivers, they will not sweep over you. When you walk through the fire, you will not be burned; the flames will not set you ablaze.   ~ Isaiah 43:2

But this I call to mind, and therefore I have hope: The steadfast love of the LORD never ceases, his mercies never come to an end; they are new every morning; great is thy faithfulness.

~ Lamentations 3:21-23

* * *

Come to me, all you who are weary and burdened and I will give you rest.

~ Matthew 11:28

With man this is impossible, but with God all things are possible.

~ Matthew 19:26

"What do you want me to do for you?" Jesus asked.

~ Mark 10:51

And we know that all things work together for good to those who love God, to those who are the called according to His purpose.

~ Romans 8:28

Be joyful in hope, patient in affliction, faithful in prayer.

~ Romans 12:12

It always protects, always trusts, always hopes, always
perseveres... Love never fails. ...And now these three remain:
faith, hope and love. But the greatest of these is love.

~ 1 Corinthians 13: 7,8,13

Now to Him who is able to do immeasurably more than all
we ask or imagine, according to His power that is at work
within us, to Him be glory in the church and in Christ Jesus
throughout all generations, for ever and ever! Amen.

~ Ephesians 3:20-21

Do not be anxious about anything, but in every situation,
by prayer and petition, with thanksgiving, present your
requests to God. And the peace of God, which transcends all
understanding, will guard your hearts and your minds in Christ
Jesus.   ~ Philippians 4:6-7

And without faith it is impossible to please God, because
anyone who comes to him must believe that he exists and that
he rewards those who earnestly seek him.   ~ Hebrews 11:6

If any of you lacks wisdom, you should ask God, who gives
generously to all without finding fault, and it will be given to
you.   ~ James 1:5

Armor of God

Finally, be strong in the Lord and in his mighty power. Put on the full armor of God, so that you can take your stand against the devil's schemes. For our struggle is not against flesh and blood, but against the rulers, against the authorities, against the powers of this dark world and against the spiritual forces of evil in the heavenly realms. Therefore put on the full armor of God, so that when the day of evil comes, you may be able to stand your ground, and after you have done everything, to stand. Stand firm then, with the belt of truth buckled around your waist, with the breastplate of righteousness in place, and with your feet fitted with the readiness that comes from the gospel of peace. In addition to all this, take up the shield of faith, with which you can extinguish all the flaming arrows of the evil one. Take the helmet of salvation and the sword of the Spirit, which is the word of God. And pray in the Spirit on all occasions with all kinds of prayers and requests. With this in mind, be alert and always keep on praying for all the Lord's people. ~ Ephesians 6:10-18

* * *

On July 13, 2019, at God's Golden Thread conference in Hayden, Idaho, where Bill and I were featured speakers, these scripture verses were spoken over Bill as both Bill and I were presented with new "walking sticks" created from a burled tree limb. Originally, it was one branch but separated into two walking sticks – one for each of us. We were both supported by God as we choose to abide in Him. ("I am the vine; you are the branches. If you remain in me and I in you, you will bear much fruit; apart from me you can do nothing." ~ John 15:5)

Yea, though I walk through the valley of the shadow of death, I will fear no evil; for you are with me: Your rod and Your staff they comfort me.   ~ Psalm 23:4

For you have delivered my soul from death, My eyes from tears, And my feet from falling. I will walk before the Lord in the land of the living.   ~ Psalm 116:8-9

Acknowledgements

First and foremost, God deserves all the praise and honor and glory for guiding us through this life adventure. Bill and I wouldn't have made it without Him.

To our family and church family, and friends, your prayers and words of encouragement kept us afloat.

Pastors Dave and Alice Darroch, thank you for your prayers and for standing and believing for the miracles we saw God do countless times.

Christine Dupre, Bill's favorite New England Patriots fan, you are a book cover designer extraordinaire.

Russ Davis, Gray Dog Press, thank you for helping me make my book dreams come true.

A special thanks to Andrea, Cherelle, Kelly, and Mary who have walked with me on my own health adventure, I will be forever grateful.

The Man Behind
the Dreams, Visions & Miracles

William "Bill" F. Hollace Jr.

Born in Malden, Massachusetts on a hot summer day, August 28, 1943, Bill remained an East Coast boy at heart until his final breath. A New England Patriots fan transplanted in the middle of Seattle Seahawks country, Bill was loyal to his New England roots.

Bill proudly served his country as a United States Marine. The expression, "Once a Marine, always a Marine" definitely was true in Bill's life. His ability to know the time without looking at a clock was amazing and "Semper Fi" – Always Faithful – defined how he lived his life.

"Bill could see the good in someone that no one else could see" is a fitting tribute to Bill's ability to encourage and challenge others. Bill and his wife, Barbara, spent almost 12 years serving the homeless and low-income population in Spokane, Washington as homeless shelter and apartment managers. It was a labor of love as they helped those who had fallen through the cracks find new hope and healing.

In the last several years, some major health issues redefined his life. But time and time again, Bill rallied from near death to conquer another medical mountain. Bill was fondly called the "Miracle Man" as God saved Bill's life many times. Bill and Barbara gave others hope as they followed his journey to healing. Their love for each other was a bright light wherever they went. Love never fails!

His contagious laughter, witty sense of humor, and kind heart sometimes were masked by a "tough" exterior as Bill made security his business. Bill was a volunteer with the S.C.O.P.E. [Sheriff Community-Oriented Policing Effort] program in Spokane Valley, Washington. A member of Spokane Dream Center, Bill was often found at the door greeting those who entered and keeping a watchful eye out for trouble, keeping others safe was important to Bill.

Bill's final greeting as you left his presence was often, "Be safe. Stay out of Trouble."

Once a Marine, Always a Marine

There are many things in our lives that shape our outlook, perspective, approach to life, and even our attitude. For many men and women, the time spent in military training and service forever changes the course of their lives.

The discipline, commitment, perseverance, and courage that is required to serve in the U.S. Military is a high calling that has been passed down through generations. As a nation, may we continue to honor those who so valiantly served, and those who are currently serving, to defend our country and its citizens.

Bill was proud to be a United States Marine. "Semper Fidelis" – which is Latin for Always Faithful, is a code Bill lived by as he cared for me and for others God brought into his life.

It was fun to listen to the banter between men who served in other branches of the service. There is a bond, a brotherhood that is undeniable. They could kid around with each other, but God help the "outsider" who tried to pick on one of their own.

Bill's faith in God was the rudder of his ship as he navigated the stormy waters of his illness. But I also believe that Bill's training as a Marine cultivated the fighting spirit that helped him rise up and out of the pit where an illness tried to contain him.

I am blessed to be the wife of a U.S. Marine. One of our friends who served in the Air Force dubbed me an "honorary Marine" for my service to Bill during his healing journey. What an honor and privilege to serve the one you love in their time of need.

The Marine Corps anthem includes a line about United States Marines guarding the streets of heaven. I believe my dear husband is one of those God called home to a new duty station.

Once a Marine, always a Marine.

Semper Fi! Oo-rah!

About the Author

Barbara Hollace

Barbara Hollace is a Christian woman who loves the Lord. God has called her to be a prayer warrior and a writer. Her greatest joy is to pray for others and see God's miracles happen. Through her own husband's health challenges, Barbara learned that prayer can move mountains in our lives.

Her love of writing blossomed from an early age when she started creating her own greeting cards for family and friends. In 1985, Barbara self-published her first poetry book, "From Dust to Dust." Since that time Barbara has been published in 20 books [as author or contributing author] as well as numerous newspaper articles. She has written 15 novels and is pursuing publication options.

Professionally, she is an author, editor, writing coach, and speaker. Owner of Hollace Writing Services, Barbara's goal is to "identify the good and magnify it!" This includes helping a person get the story in their heart on the page, editing the story, and pursuing publication options. She recently opened her own publishing company, Hollace House Publishing, and will be expanding its reach in the upcoming years.

Barbara has a Bachelor's degree in Business Administration from Western Washington University and a Juris Doctor degree from Gonzaga University School of Law. She is also the Communications Director for Spokane Dream Center church in Spokane Valley, Washington.

For more information about Barbara and her business, go to www.barbarahollace.com.

Author's Note

How was your adventure? My prayer is that as you followed along with Bill's adventure, our adventure, that you were blessed. Whether you walked this initial path with us, or if you are new to our story, God has been drawing you to this connection for a long time.

Bill and I are just ordinary people who love and serve an extraordinary God. Your heavenly Father wants to talk with you. The truth is God is talking to us all the time, the noise in our lives keeps us from hearing Him.

It's been a blessing to open the curtain and give you a peek inside our adventure. When you encounter the glory of God, you can't keep it to yourself.

As I walk through my own health journey, daily I am so grateful for God's love. I am filled with hope and joy as I abide in God's presence.

Now to Him who is able to do immeasurably more than all we ask or imagine, according to His power that is at work within us, to Him be glory in the church and in Christ Jesus throughout all generations, for ever and ever! Amen. (Ephesians 3:20-21 NIV)

Other Books

Barbara Hollace, Contributing Author

- *Light for the Writer's Soul: 100 Devotions by Global Christian Writers*: Armour Publishers
- *Love, Animals and Miracles*: New World Library
- *Gonzaga Book of Prayer*: Gonzaga University
- *A Miracle under the Christmas Tree*: Harlequin
- *And Then What Happened*: CreateSpace
- *Love is a Verb Devotional*: Bethany House
- *A Book of Miracles*: New World Library
- *Faith, Hope and Healing*: John Wiley and Sons
- *SpokeWrite: Journal of Art and Writing* (3 issues): Gray Dog Press
- *A Cup of Comfort for Military Families*: Adams Media
- *Mistletoe Madness*: Blooming Tree Press
- *God's Words for the Young*: Choat &Lederman
- *The Art of Brave Living*: Diane Cunningham
- *Divine Interventions: Heartwarming Stories of Answered Prayer*: Guideposts

Our Story for His Glory

Few of us have the honor and privilege of sharing our story in our lifetime. Being alive is a great testimony of God's miraculous work in your life. MultiCare Hospital was launching two new programs: The Pulse Heart Institute and Neuroscience Institute and featured Bill's story to help roll them out.

Use the QR code below to access a short video about Bill's adventure. You get to hear the voice behind the story. Enjoy!

Made in United States
Troutdale, OR
11/19/2023